MATERIALS

By

Steffi Cavell-Clarke

©2017
Book Life
King's Lynn
Norfolk PE30 4LS

ISBN: 978-1-78637-144-7

Written by:
Steffi Cavell-Clarke

Edited by:
Charlie Ogden

Designed by:
Danielle Rippengill

A catalogue record for this book
is available from the British Library

PHOTO CREDITS

Abbreviations: l-left, r-right, b-bottom, t-top, c-centre, m-middle.

Front cover – LuckyImages. 2 – Sergey Novikov. 4 – Brian A Jackson. 5– Tom Wang. 6 – Sergey Nivens. 7tl – Pawel Michalowski. 7tr – ESOlex. 7bl – 10 FACE. 7bm – sigurcamp. 7br – Vladitto. 8 – All For You. 9t – MO_SES Premium. 9b – James Steidl. 10l – Dmitry Polonskiy. 10m – Yuri Kabantsev. 10r – martinho Smart. 11 – SOMMAI. 12 – Alexandr Makarov. 13 – photka. 14 – Photosebia. 15 – Kevin Penhallow. 16 – Gelpi. 17 – Luis Molinero. 18l – Evgeny Karandaev. 18r – O.Bellini. 19 – Alexander Dotsenko. 20 – isak55. 21 – Valua Vitaly. 22tl – ILYA AKINSHIN. 22tr – studiovin. 22bl – Bernd Schmidt. 22br – Fat Jackey. 23 – Oksana Kuzmina
Images are courtesy of Shutterstock.com.
With thanks to Getty Images, Thinkstock Photo and iStockphoto.

CONTENTS

Words that look like **this** can be found in the glossary on page 24.

What Is SCIENCE?

Why does water turn into ice?

What are cars and aeroplanes made from?

Where does wood come from?

Science can answer many difficult questions we may have and help us to understand the world around us.

5

What Are MATERIALS?

Materials are what **objects** are made of and they are all around us. We use lots of different materials every day.

There are many different kinds of material. Plastic, rock, glass, metal and wood are some of the most common types of material.

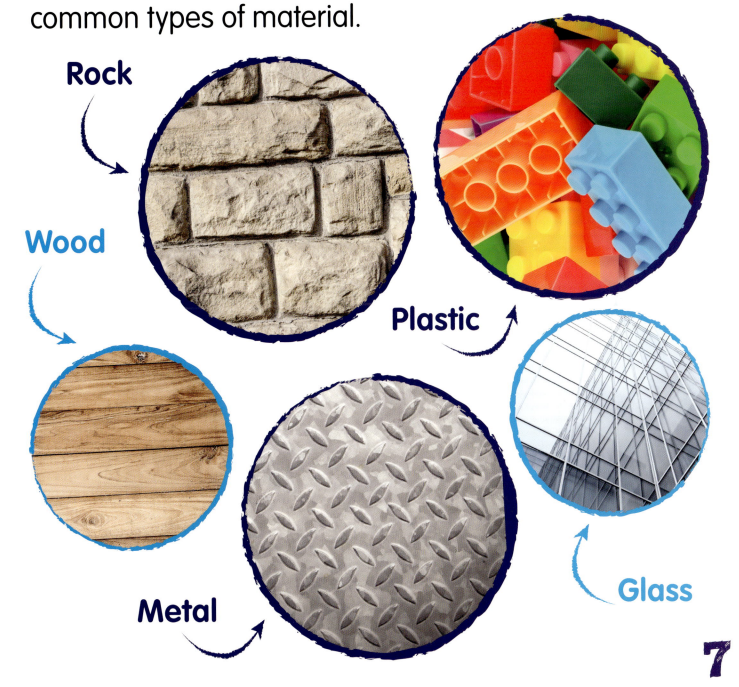

Rock

Wood

Plastic

Metal

Glass

7

HARD AND SOFT

Fabric

Different types of material are used for different things. Soft materials, such as fabrics, are used to make clothes.

Hard and strong materials are used to make large objects, such as aeroplanes and buses.

Aeroplane

Bus

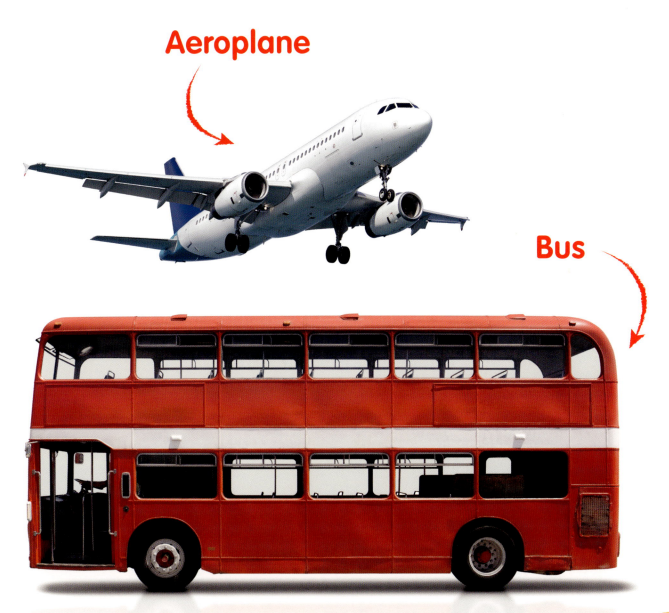

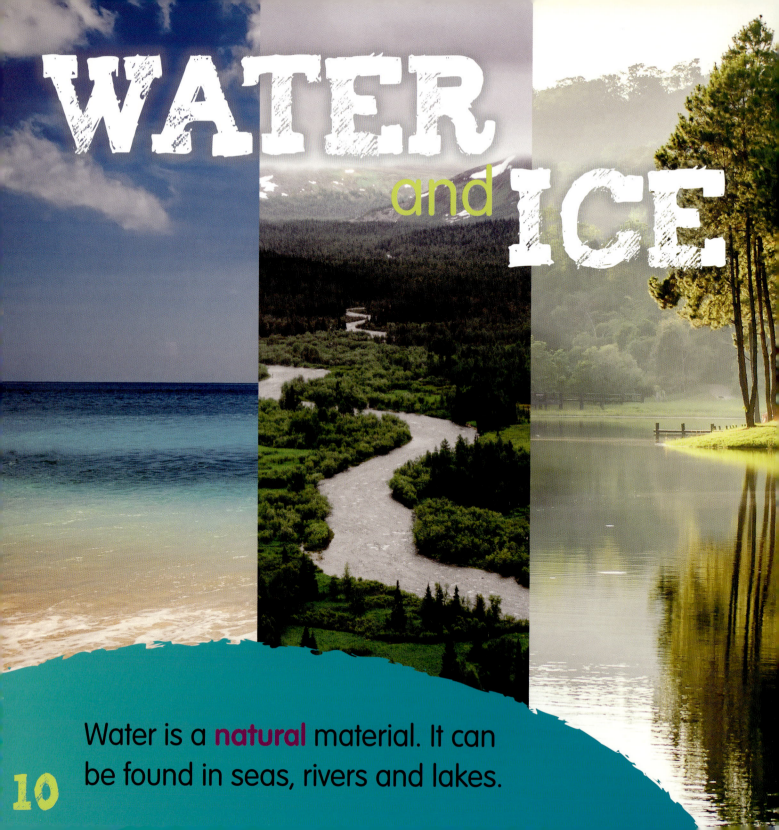

WATER and ICE

Water is a **natural** material. It can be found in seas, rivers and lakes.

Water is a **liquid**. When water gets very cold it turns into ice, which is a **solid**.

Ice

PLASTIC

Plastic is a **man-made** material. Plastic can be made into almost any shape. Plastic is strong but if it gets very hot, it will start to melt.

12

Plastic is used to make many toys and games because it is light and strong. Buckets and spades are often made of plastic.

Spade

Bucket

ROCK

Rock is a natural material that is found all over planet Earth. Rock is strong, hard and solid.

Many houses are built using rock. Roofs are often covered in slate, which is a type of rock.

Slate

GLASS

Glass is a solid, man-made material that is made using sand. Glass is see–though and it usually feels smooth.

Strong glass is used to make the windows in houses. It can also be used to make bottles and jars.

Glass can be **recycled**.

METAL

Steel and iron are strong.

Aluminium is flexible and light.

Metals are natural, shiny materials that are found in rocks. There are many different types of metal.

Cars, bikes and aeroplanes are all made from metal. Steel and iron are so strong that they are used to make buildings and bridges.

19

WOOD

Wood is a natural material that comes from trees. Some types of wood are very light and others are very strong and heavy.

Wood is used to make paper and cardboard. Other things are also made of wood, such as instruments and pencils.

This guitar is made of wood.

Let's
EXPERIMENT!

Do you know which materials are man-made?
Let's find out!

YOU WILL NEED:

Five pence piece
Feather
Plastic straw
Wooden spoon
Pencil
Glass bottle

STEP 1

Place all the objects in front of you.

STEP 2

Pick up each object. What does it feel like?
Is it hard or soft?

STEP 3

What do you think the object is made of? Do you think it is made of a natural or man-made material?

TOP TIP: Ask an adult to help you!

RESULTS:

Man-made material: plastic straw, glass bottle
Natural material: five pence piece, feather,
wooden spoon, pencil

23

GLOSSARY

flexible   easy to bend

liquid   a material that flows, such as water

man-made   not natural, made by humans

natural   found in nature, not man-made

objects   things that can be seen and touched

recycled   used again to make something else

solid   firm and stable, not a liquid

INDEX